Let's Explore
Solids

by Anne J. Spaight

BUMBA BOOKS™

LERNER PUBLICATIONS ◆ MINNEAPOLIS

Note to Educators:

Throughout this book, you'll find critical thinking questions. These can be used to engage young readers in thinking critically about the topic and in using the text and photos to do so.

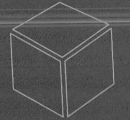

Lerner Publications Company
A division of Lerner Publishing Group, Inc.
241 First Avenue North
Minneapolis, MN 55401 USA

For reading levels and more information, look up this title at www.lernerbooks.com.

Library of Congress Cataloging-in-Publication Data

Names: Spaight, Anne J., 1983– author.
Title: Let's explore solids / by Anne J. Spaight.
Description: Minneapolis : Lerner Publications, [2018] | Series: Bumba books.
   A first look at physical science | Audience: Ages 4–7. | Audience: K to Grade 3.
   | Includes bibliographical references and index.
Identifiers: LCCN 2017024975 (print) | LCCN 2017019801 (ebook) | ISBN
   9781512482768 (eb pdf) | ISBN 9781512482669 (lb : alk. paper) | ISBN
   9781541510852 (pb : alk. paper)
Subjects: LCSH: Solids—Properties—Juvenile literature. |
   Matter—Properties—Juvenile literature.
Classification: LCC QC176.3 (print) | LCC QC176.3 .S65 2018 (ebook) | DDC
   530.4/1—dc23

LC record available at https://lccn.loc.gov/2017024975

Manufactured in the United States of America
1 – CG – 12/31/17

Expand learning beyond the printed book. Download free, complementary educational resources for this book from our website, www.lernerresource.com.

Table of Contents

What Are Solids?

Matter is all around us.

Solids are one type of matter.

Gases and liquids are also matter.

Solids are hard matter

we can see.

We can see liquids too.

We cannot see most gases.

What solids can you see at the beach? What liquids can you see?

Solids take up space.

You can touch them.

Structures at the park are solids. What other objects outside are solids?

Solids keep their shape.

Solids do not flow.

You can cut a solid.

You can shape it.

It will stay that shape.

Can you think of other solids you can shape?

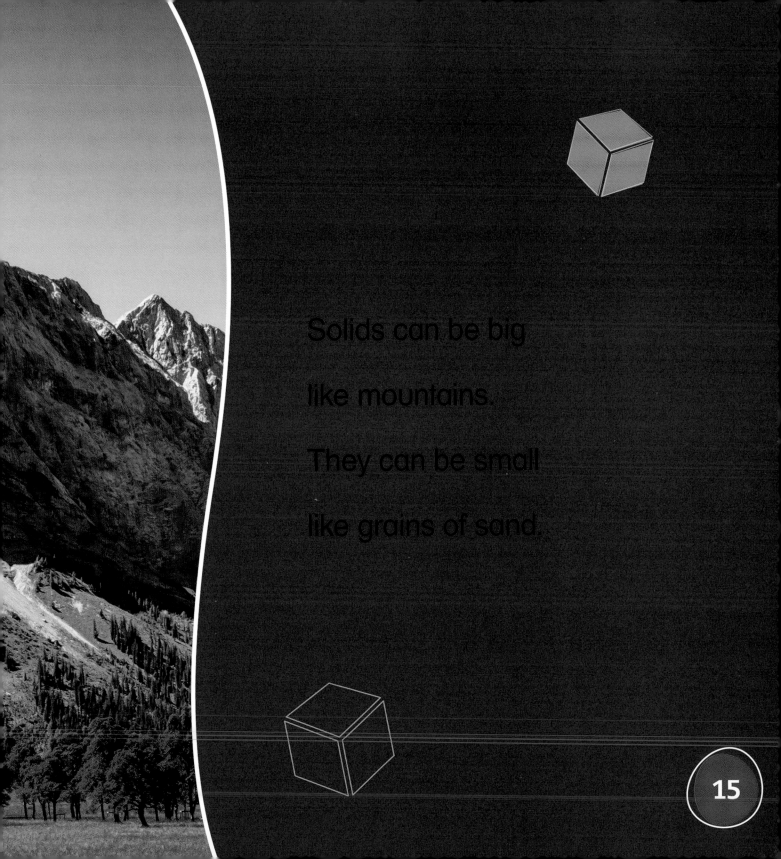

Solids can be big

like mountains.

They can be small

like grains of sand.

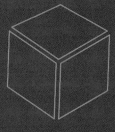

Some solids are hard like rocks.

Others are soft like feathers.

Solids can melt into liquid.

Ice melts into water.

Candles melt into wax.

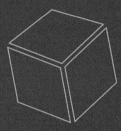

Solids are all around you.

What solids can you see and touch?

Picture Quiz

Which of these pictures show solids?

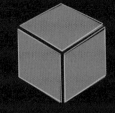

Picture Glossary

gases

things such as air that spread to fill any space that contains them

liquids

things that flow and can be poured

matter

something that takes up space or has weight

melt

to turn from a solid to a liquid

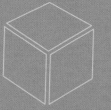

Read More

Hansen, Amy S. *Matter Comes in All Shapes.* North Mankato, MN: Rourke Publishing, 2012.

Hoffmann, Sara E. *Solids.* Minneapolis: LernerClassroom, 2013.

Montgomery, Anne. *Solid or Liquid?* Huntington Beach, CA: Teacher Created Materials, 2015.

Index

Photo Credits